Heart Speaks to Heart

Heart Speaks to Heart

Three Gospel Meditations on Jesus

HENRI J.M. NOUWEN
foreword by Christopher de Vinck

ave maria press **AMP** notre dame, indiana

First printing, January 1989
First revised edition, March 2007
57,000 copies in print

Excerpts from *The New Jerusalem Bible*, copyright © 1985 by Darton, Longman & Todd, Ltd. and Doubleday & Company, Inc. Reprinted by permission of the publisher.

Founded in 1865, Ave Maria Press is a ministry of the Indiana Province of Holy Cross.

www.avemariapress.com

ISBN-10 1-59471-116-X ISBN-13 978-1-59471-116-9

Cover and text design by David R. Scholtes

Printed and bound in the United States of America.

Contents

Foreword

From our birth to our death, we walk on the journey toward Jerusalem. Season to season we advance, often in conformity and comfort, often in turmoil and pain. Along the way no one is blind to the labor: schedules, school, paychecks, boredom, regrets, flowers in the garden, pumpkins on the stoop. We tend to create habits of living that provide us with what we need in order to survive. But we are also searching . . . searching for peace. It is a journey toward Jerusalem.

Henri Nouwen believed, as is clearly written in this little book, that our survival depends upon this search for peace, and at the root of that search lies our universal desire to be loved. In these pages, you will hear him explain that we already know the love we desire, but we cannot easily define it to others. Henri spent his life trying to define this love to his family and friends, to his students, and to his readers. He did not focus on the sorrows, but celebrated the joys in the context of sorrow.

In the three prayers that constitute *Heart Speaks to Heart: Three Gospel Meditations on Jesus*, Henri suggests that as we walk through the circuit of daily routines, we can forget the universal recognition of loneliness and separation. In our journey, we often forget God and are distracted. Or, if we seek beyond God, we find ourselves in the midst of loss. Henri reminds us that it is in the union of those we love that we find salvation. There we abandon loneliness. There we end the devastation of separation. That love, Henri wrote, ultimately is the love given and received from God.

At the end of Archibald MacLeish's play *JB*, the play about the courage of Job to maintain his faith, MacLeish suggests that if we blow on the coal of the heart we will maintain our faith and hope for the future. Henri always maintained that such are the habits of faithful people. He would say heart needs to speak to heart. All of his books can be seen as asking us: How do we maintain the fire within us? How do we tend to the hope of self in the face of our lost selves?

We find Henri's answer in these pages: by experiencing the "healing and renewing love that flows from the heart of Jesus." And he reminds us that such love can be felt from the embrace of another human being.

Henri clearly understood the paradox of discovering strength in the broken heart. He understood the need to be vulnerable in order to receive love. He defined the doubts we possess in the presence of the resurrection, and such certitude can be found, as well, in the works of Thomas Merton, C. S. Lewis, and Teilhard de Chardin.

A prophet is nothing more than a person who has a broad view and can interpret and explain the consequences of our faith or our lack of faith. Henri Nouwen was one of the holiest men I have known, perhaps a prophet, surely an ordinary man with an extraordinary gift to explain the joys of a living Christ. Henri understood the habits of the soul and lived in the order of spiritual justice that exists when placed in the court of a merciful God. He reminds us in these meditations that even in the ruination of our stupidity we find the markings of the way back to peace. After the darkness, there is light. After the hunger, there is food. After the loneliness, there is companionship. After the wound, there is healing. After death, there is life.

If we blow on the coal of our hearts, there will be a flame and a light, which, as Henri so believed, can ignite in us the awareness of an unconditional love that is holy and eternal.

Christopher de Vinck
editor of *Nouwen Then: Personal Reflections of Henri*
author of *The Power of the Powerless: A Brother's Legacy of Love*
Pompton Plains, New Jersey

Prologue

This little book of prayers has its own unique story.

From August 1985 until July 1986, I lived in Trosly, France, as part of a l'Arche community. L'Arche is a worldwide network of communities where mentally handicapped people and their assistants try to live together in the spirit of the Beatitudes. It was founded in 1964 by the Canadian Jean Vanier and the French Dominican Thomas Philippe, in the little village of Trosly-Breuil.

When I arrived in Trosly, I was given a room in the house of Madame Pauline Vanier, one of the most vibrant, articulate and spirited people I have ever met. She is the mother of Jean Vanier and the widow of Georges Vanier, former Governor General of Canada. Becoming friends with "Mammie" Vanier was one of the special graces of my year in Trosly, and that friendship led me to write these prayers.

It all began with an icon Robert Lentz had made for me portraying John the Evangelist leaning against Jesus' breast in the heavenly Jerusalem. Called "The

Bridegroom," the icon best expresses my own desire to develop a more intimate relationship with Jesus.

I had some large photographs made of the work and had one of them framed as a Christmas gift for Mammie. She not only loved the icon and gave it a special place in her living room, but she also expressed her gratitude by telling me about her deep devotion to the heart of Jesus.

Even though I was in search of a deeper personal relationship with Jesus, I had never felt any great desire to pray to the "Sacred Heart." Nineteenth-century piety and the statues in which that piety was expressed had kept me away from the devotion that for many people had been very nurturing. I was quite hesitant, therefore, when Mammie Vanier brought up the subject. But the way she spoke to me about it was different from what I expected.

She told me about Pére Almire Pichon, S.J. This Jesuit was for a while the spiritual director of Thérèse of Lisieux. He had also been the spiritual director of Pauline Vanier's mother and had implanted in her heart and mind a solid and deep devotion to the

Sacred Heart. For her, Almire Pichon was a true man of God, deeply immersed in the mystery of the Sacred Heart. Mammie remembered this saintly man quite well and was convinced that her own deep devotion to the Sacred Heart was given to her by her mother and Père Pichon.

Sometime later, when we were speaking about this again, she said with great conviction and with an obvious tremble in her voice, "Henri, I know for sure that God wants you to write about the Sacred Heart." I was somewhat taken aback and I did not hide my hesitation. "Well," I said, "I don't think I can do it, it just doesn't seem the right thing for me. There is nothing in me that feels inspired to write about the Sacred Heart."

She dropped the subject, but not long afterward she came to my room on the second floor, something she had never done before. Since she was eighty-seven years old and had a hard time walking, her climb to my room required a very special effort and a very special reason. As she sat down on the little wooden chair near my table, she said, "Henri, the thought that you should write about the Sacred Heart does not leave me. I know for sure it is not just the silly idea of an old lady, but a real inspiration that came to me."

The fierceness in her eyes and the authority in her voice made me realize that this was not the moment to be flippant. So I said, "I hear you, and I am taking very seriously what you say, but I have to say to you that I have no idea how and when I can do it."

She smiled and said, "Well, you will know, and I will keep reminding you. I am a stubborn old lady, after all, and I am not afraid to push you a little, especially when I know that what I tell you comes from God."

I started to laugh and said, "I know you will keep after me. I promise you to keep listening, but you have to be patient." She looked at me with her very caring, but also very determined, look and said, "I can't be too patient because I'm not a young woman anymore, and I would like to see it finished before the Lord calls me home!"

After that memorable visit, we developed a little game in which she would say, "Henri, have you not forgotten?" and I would answer, "No, I haven't, but it isn't the time yet." Later, when I had moved to Toronto and we spoke occasionally by phone, she kept saying, "Have you not forgotten?" and sometimes mutual friends came to visit me and said that they didn't know what it meant, but Mammie told them to ask me whether I had forgotten.

My own life became busier, especially after I had decided to move to Daybreak, the l'Arche community in Toronto, and to live and work there as their priest. Time for writing was minimal, and writing about the heart of Jesus seemed further and further from my mind.

But then, physical and emotional exhaustion forced me to take a long time off. I left Daybreak and went to a community in Winnipeg, Manitoba, to look for healing and new strength. As Holy Week approached, I felt a strong desire to celebrate the passion and resurrection of Jesus in deep solitude. I asked the Trappists in Holland, Manitoba, if I could join them for Holy Week and Easter. As I prepared for my time with them, Mammie's words came back to me. I called my friend, Annice Callahan, R.S.C.J., who had written extensively about the Sacred Heart, and asked her to send me some books on the subject. She graciously sent me a whole box of literature, which I took with me to the monastery. Holy Week seemed the right time to write about the heart of Jesus.

Well, it was and it wasn't! As soon as I was settled in the monastery, I realized that I had come there to be silent and to pray, and not to study the latest books about the Sacred Heart. I knew it wouldn't work. During the early days of Holy Week, I did some reading, especially the texts on the heart of Christ written by Pedro Arrupe, S.J., when he was the Superior General of the Society of Jesus. The collection, entitled *In Him Alone Is Our Hope*, moved me deeply and stirred up a new desire to enter more fully into the mystery of God's love as lived out in the passion and resurrection of Jesus.

But something had changed in me. I no longer wanted to write about the heart of Jesus. In my own heart I began to discern a real desire to speak to the heart of Jesus and be heard. Somehow Madame Vanier's call no longer seemed a call to write a contemporary interpretation of the devotion to the Sacred Heart, but an invitation to let the heart of Jesus touch my own heart deeply and to be healed by that experience.

The pain of having to leave Daybreak for a time, and not being able to be there during Holy Week and Easter, cut very deep in my heart. At some moments, it seemed hardly tolerable. But as I looked up to Jesus, washing his disciples' feet and sharing with them his body and blood; being beaten, crowned with thorns and nailed on the cross; appearing to his disciples and showing them the wounds in his hands, feet and side, I knew that I had come to pray and let my wounds become one with the wounds of my crucified and risen Lord.

When Holy Thursday came, I began to write to Jesus—from heart to heart. I also wrote on Good Friday and on Easter Sunday. I did not look at any article or book. I simply prayed as I wrote and wrote as I prayed. It was easy; it came without effort. The words just flowed out of me, and I realized that I was doing precisely what Mammie had hoped for from the very beginning. She wanted me to pray and to pray with my whole heart, and she knew that the heart of Jesus would open my heart for such prayer.

I

"Come to me . . ."

"Come to me, all you who labor and are overburdened, and I will give you rest. Shoulder my yoke and learn from me, for I am gentle and humble in heart, and you will find rest for your souls. Yes, my yoke is easy and my burden light."

—Matthew 11:28–30

Dear Lord Jesus,

You, the eternal Word, through whom all things came into being, you became flesh among us so that you could speak with us, walk with us, pray with us, yes even die with us. You became a human being among other human beings so that nothing human would be alien to you, so that in everything, except sin, you could be like us.

By so doing, you showed us the immense love of the One who sent you, your heavenly Father. Through your human heart we can catch a glimpse of the divine love with which we are loved and with which you yourself love us, because you and your Father are one.

It is so hard for me to believe fully in the love that flows from your heart. I am so insecure, so fearful, so doubtful and so distrustful. While I say with my words that I believe in your full and unconditional love, I continue to look for affection, support, acceptance and praise among my fellow human beings, always expecting from them what only you can give.

I clearly hear your voice saying, "Come to me you who labor and are overburdened . . . for I am gentle and humble in heart," and yet I run off in other directions as if I did not trust you and feel somehow safer in the company of people whose hearts are divided and often confused.

O Lord, why is it that I am so eager to receive human praise and human support even when experience tells me how limited and conditional is the love that comes from a human heart? So many people have shown me their love and affection; so many have given me words of affirmation and encouragement; so many have been generous and forgiving toward me . . . but no one could touch that deep, hidden place where my fear and my loneliness dwell.

Only you know that place, Lord. It is hidden even from me, and only in moments of great anguish and pain do I become aware of it. Then I realize how very lonely I am, marked by a loneliness that cannot be removed by any other sinful human being. My deepest loneliness can only awaken the same loneliness in others and create fear and anguish there, instead of love and healing. My own anguish calls forth anguish in others. It reminds them of their own emptiness and isolation. It makes them aware that there is not enough space in them to embrace their fellow human beings. One human loneliness cannot heal the other.

Your heavenly Father saw the desperation of humanity. He saw the greed, lust, anger, resentment, violence and destruction with which we, your people, tried to find a way to peace and harmony. Instead of this peace, we found only conflict and war.

But your Father's love was so unlimited that he wanted us to know that love and to find in it the fulfillment of our deepest desires. So, he sent us you, with a human heart big enough to hold all human loneliness and all human anguish. Your heart is not a heart of stone, but a heart of flesh; your heart of flesh is not narrowed by human sin and unfaithfulness, but is as wide and deep as divine love itself. Your heart does not distinguish between rich and poor, friend and enemy, female and male, slave and free, sinner and saint. Your heart is open to receive anyone with total, unrestricted love. For anyone who wants to come to you, there is room. You want to draw all people to yourself and offer them a home where every human desire is met, every human longing comes to rest and every human need is satisfied.

But your heart is gentle and humble. You do not force; you do not pull or push; you do not coerce. You want us to come freely to your heart and trust that we will find there the peace and joy we most desire. You do not put any requirement on us; you do not expect any great act of generosity; you do not hope for heroic gestures or dramatic signs. The only thing you want is trust. You can only give your heart to those who come to it in trust.

It is you who reach out first. You said it so clearly, "You did not choose me; no, I chose you." Your choosing us is your great act of trust. You trusted that in our sinful, broken and vulnerable heart lies the potential to reach out to your heart and say, "Lord, to whom shall we go? You have the message of eternal life and we believe; we have come to know that you

24

are the holy one of God." All that you hope for is our simple, trusting "yes."

You did everything to show us your love and your Father's love. You became a small, dependent child to show us yourself in your weakness; you became a refugee in Egypt to show us your solidarity with all who are driven from their homes; you grew up in obedience to your parents to show us how close you are as we search for a true identity; you worked for many years as a simple carpenter to show us how you wanted to be with us in our daily work; you were tempted in the desert to show us how to resist the forces of evil around us; you surrounded yourself with disciples to show us how to share our vision with others and to work together in ministry; you preached the word of God to show us your truth and how to become, ourselves, witnesses to truth; you healed the sick and raised the dead to show us that your presence gave life to the whole person, body and soul; you were transfigured to show us your divine splendor; you went the long road of suffering and death to show us that you did not want to remain an outsider even in the most painful of all human experiences. You, the eternal Word of the Father, kept making choices that brought you closer and closer to us, to reveal to us the boundless love of your heart.

O Lord, all you ask of me is a simple "yes," a simple act of trust, so that your choices for me can bear fruit in my life. I do not want you to pass me by. I do not want to be so busy with my way of living, my plans and projects, my relatives, friends and acquaintances, that I do not even notice that you are with me, closer to me than anyone else. I do not want to be blind to the loving gestures that come from your hands, nor deaf to the caring words that come from your mouth. I want to see you as you walk with me and hear you as you speak to me.

Your heart is so full of the desire to love me, so aflame with a fire to warm me. You so much want to give me a home, a sense of belonging, a place to dwell, a shelter where I feel protected and a refuge in which I feel safe. You stand at so many squares and corners of my life and say with so much tenderness, "Come and see, come and stay with me. When you are thirsty, come to me . . . you who put your trust in me, come and drink. Come, you who are tired, exhausted, depressed, discouraged and dispirited. Come, you who feel pain in your body, fatigue in your anxious mind and doubt and anguish in the depth of your heart. Come and know that I have come to give you a new heart and a new spirit, yes, even a new body in which the struggles of your life can be seen as signs of beauty and hope. Come to me and trust me. In my Father's house there are many places to live. I am going now to prepare a place for you, and, after I have gone and prepared you a place, I will return and take you to myself so that you may be where I am."

I hear your words, Jesus. I want to hear them with my whole being so that your words can become flesh in me and form a dwelling place for you. Help me to close the many doors and windows of my heart through which I flee from you or through which I give entry to words and sounds coming not from you, but from a raging, screaming world that wants to pull me away from you.

I am looking at you, Lord. You have said so many loving words. Your heart has spoken so clearly. Now you want to show me even more clearly how much you love me. Knowing that your Father has put everything in your hands, that you have come from God and are returning to God, you remove your outer garments and, taking a towel, you wrap it around your waist, pour water into a basin and begin to wash my feet, and then wipe them with the towel you are wearing.

O Lord, you kneel before me; you hold my naked feet in your hands, and you look up at me and smile. Within me I feel the protest arising, "No, Lord, you shall never wash my feet." It is as if I were resisting the love you offer me. I want to say, "You don't really know me, my dark feelings, my pride, my lust, my greed. I may speak the right words, but my heart is so far from you. No, I am not good enough to belong to you. You must have someone else in mind, not me." But you look at me with utter tenderness, saying, "I want you to be with me. I want you to have a full share in my life. I want you to belong to me as much as I belong to my Father. I want to wash you completely clean so that you and I can be one and so that you can do to others what I have done to you." I have to let go of all my fears, distrust, doubts and anguish and simply let you wash me clean and make me your friend whom you love with a love that has no bounds.

I am looking at you again, Lord. You stand up and invite me to the table. As we are eating, you take bread, say the blessing, break the bread and give it to me. "Take and eat," you say, "this is my body given for you." Then you take a cup, and, after giving thanks, you hand it to me, saying, "This is my blood, the blood of the new covenant poured out for you." Knowing that your hour has come to pass from this world to your Father and having loved me, you now love me to the end. You give me everything that you have and are. You pour out for me your very self. All the love that you carry for me in your heart now becomes manifest. You wash my feet and then give me your own body and blood as food and drink.

O Lord, how can I ever go anywhere else but to you to find the love I so desire! How can I expect from people as sinful as myself a love that can touch me in the most hidden corners of my being? Who can wash me clean as you do and give me food and drink as you do? Who wants me to be so close, so intimate and so safe as you do? O Lord, your love is not an intangible love, a love that remains words and thoughts. No, Lord, your love is a love that comes from your human heart. It is a heart-felt love that expresses itself through your whole being. You speak . . . you look . . . you touch . . . you give me food. Yes, you make your love a love that reaches all the senses of my body and holds me as a mother holds her child, embraces me as a father embraces his son and touches me as a brother touches his sister and brother.

O dear Jesus, your heart is only love. I see you; I hear you; I touch you. With all my being, I know that you love me.

I trust in you, Lord, but keep helping me in my many moments of distrust and doubt. They are there and will be there every time I turn my eyes, ears or hands away from you. Please, Lord, keep calling me back to you, by day and by night, in joy and in sadness, during moments of success and moments of failure. Never let me leave you. I know you walk with me. Help me walk with you today, tomorrow and always.

II

The soldier

"pierced his side with a lance . . ."

It was the Day of Preparation, and to avoid the bodies' remaining on the cross during the Sabbath—since that Sabbath was a day of special solemnity—the Jews asked Pilate to have the legs broken and the bodies taken away. Consequently the soldiers came and broke the legs of the first man who had been crucified with him and then of the other. When they came to Jesus, they saw he was already dead, and so instead of breaking his legs one of the soldiers pierced his side with a lance; and immediately there came out blood and water. This is the evidence of one who saw it—true evidence, and he knows that what he says is true—and he gives it so that you may believe as well. Because all this happened to fulfill the words of scripture:

"Not one bone of his will be broken"; and again, in another place scripture says: "They will look on the one whom they have pierced."

—John 19:31–37

Dear Lord Jesus,

You, "the image of the unseen God, the first-born of all creation, for whom all things are created in heaven and on earth, everything visible and everything invisible," you hang dead on a cross. I look at you. You have just spoken your last words, "It is fulfilled," and given up your spirit.

You have given everything. You "have emptied yourself, taking the form of a slave; you have humbled yourself by accepting death, death on a cross." Your body has been fully given for me; your blood has been fully poured out for me. You who are love have not held back anything for yourself, but have let all your love flow from your heart to make it bear fruit in me.

I look at your dead body on the cross. The soldiers, who have broken the legs of the two men crucified with you, do not break your legs, but one of them pierces your side with a lance, and immediately blood and water flow out. Your heart is broken, the heart that did not know hatred, revenge, resentment, jealousy or envy but only love, love so deep and so wide that it embraces your Father in heaven as well as all humanity in time and space. Your broken heart is the source of my salvation, the foundation of my hope, the cause of my love. It is the sacred place where all that was, is and ever shall be is held in unity. There all suffering has been suffered, all anguish lived, all loneliness endured, all abandonment felt and all agony cried out. There, human and divine love have kissed, and there God and all men and women of history are reconciled. All the tears of the human race have been cried there, all pain understood and all despair touched. Together with all people of all times, I look up to you whom they have pierced, and I gradually come to know what it means to be part of your body and your blood, what it means to be human.

O Jesus, you were sent to us not to condemn us, but to reveal to us your love and your Father's love. How much your heart wanted to give that love to me and to all people. Your only desire was that we would accept that love and let it transform us into children of your Father—your sisters and brothers. And how much you wanted to be loved. Yes, Jesus, you became vulnerable so that you could receive love from vulnerable people. You wanted to be loved by people. You wanted to be loved by those you came to save. Your heart is a heart completely open to give and receive love.

But here you are, nailed to a cross. Your heart is broken. The love you came to give was not received; the love you came to receive was not given. Your heart, that human heart overflowing with divine love, is broken. Rejected, despised, spat upon, laughed at, beaten and crowned with thorns, you hang on your cross. Those whom you encouraged with your words, set free from their demons and healed of their illnesses, are all gone. Your friend Judas betrayed you; your friend Peter denied you. No one could keep watch with you in your agony, and no one could even sense the depth of your love for them.

I look at you, Lord, and I see your pierced side, the place where your heart is broken. And as I look, my eyes begin to recognize the anguish and agony of all the people for whom you gave yourself. Your broken heart becomes the heart of all of humanity, the heart of all the world. What an anguish! What an agony! You carry them all: abandoned children, rejected wives and husbands, broken families, the homeless, refugees, prisoners, the maimed and tortured, and the thousands, yes millions, who are unloved, forgotten and left alone to die. I see their emaciated bodies, their despairing faces, their anguished looks. I see them all there, where your body is pierced and your heart is ripped apart. O compassionate Lord, your heart is broken because of all the love that is not given or received. All the people of the past, the present and those yet to be born can look up at you and see their anguish and their agony on your cross.

O dear Jesus, looking at your wounded side, I see blood and water coming out. The one who first saw it, saw it as a sign that you were the one about whom the scriptures spoke and passed on what he had seen so that I, too, might believe in you of whom no bone is broken and look up at you whom they have pierced.

Blood and water came from your pierced side. Blood and water flowed from your broken heart. Lord Jesus, help me to understand this mystery. So much blood has flowed through the centuries: blood of people who did not even know why they were trampled underfoot, mutilated, tortured, slain, beheaded and left unburied; blood caused by swords, arrows, guns and bombs, tainting the faces of millions of people; blood that comes forth from angry, bitter, jealous, vengeful hearts, and from hearts that are set on hatred, violence and destruction. From the blood of Abel killed by his brother to the blood of the Jews, the Armenians, the Ukrainians, the Irish, the Iranians and Iraqis, the Palestinians, the South Africans and the countless nations and ethnic groups victimized by the evil intentions of their sisters and brothers in the human race, blood has been covering the earth, and cries have gone up to heaven: "My God, my God, why have you forsaken us?"

O Jesus, I look into my own heart and at my own hands. There, too, I find blood. My own heart seems like a microcosm of the world of violence and destruction in which I live. I have not killed with my hands, but how well do I know the sentiments of my heart, sentiments that are no different from the sentiments of those whose circumstances led them to lash out and destroy? And can I truly say that my hands are clean? So often have they been instruments of greed and lust, of impatience and anger, of accusation and recrimination. I know that they have often been used to strike instead of caress; I know that they have often formed fists instead of making a sign of peace and reconciliation. I know how often they have taken instead of given and have pointed an accusing finger at others instead of beating my own breast. I know how often they have made signs of cursing instead of signs of peace. There is blood on my hands, too, even when I do not see it. I cannot wash my hands in innocence. Sinful, guilty and deeply ashamed, I can only stand under your cross, knowing that my hands are the hands of a blood-stained humanity.

I look at your pierced side and see blood flowing from your heart. Your heart knows no revenge, only forgiveness, no jealousy, only encouragement, no resentment, only gratitude, no hatred, only peace. Your heart is a heart where evil has no place, only love. The blood flowing from your heart is the blood of the innocent Lamb by which the sins of the world are washed away. What the blood of goats and bulls could not accomplish, your blood did accomplish. You, dear Lord, holy, spotless, innocent Lamb, are the only one who can truly offer a sacrifice to God and so enter into the heavenly sanctuary where you want to bring me with you into the presence of your Father. Your precious blood flows from your broken heart to heal my broken heart and the broken hearts of every man and woman in every time and place.

I look at your pierced side, and I see not only blood coming out, but water as well. Like blood, water too can be a sign of destruction. The great flood in Noah's time and the countless floods throughout human history show that clearly. But the water that flows from your side is a life-giving water. Not only is it a water that cleanses me from sin, but it is also water that brings me into a new land, a new home, a new community. It is the water of the Red Sea through which your people were led out of Egypt. It is the water that gushed forth from the rock in the desert to quench your people's thirst. It is the water from the Jordan through which the people and the Ark of the Covenant passed to enter into the promised land. It is the water that flowed from the Temple, becoming deeper and deeper. It is the water with which you yourself were baptized by John. It is the water that became wine at Cana. It is the healing water of the pool of Bethesda. It is the water with which you washed your disciples' feet.

Yes, Lord, the water flowing from your side is all of this, but much more than this too because it is the water by which you give us your innermost self and make us part of your communion with your Father; it is water that becomes a spring in us welling up for eternal life. Yes, Lord, the water flowing from your broken heart makes me into a new person, a child of your Father, and your brother. It is the water of baptism that has been poured over me and so many others and that has given entrance to the new community fashioned by your Spirit.

Thank you, Jesus, for the mystery of your broken heart, a heart broken by us and for us, that has become now the source of forgiveness and new life. The blood and water flowing from your side show me the new life that is given to me through your death. It is a life of intimate communion with you and your Father. But it is also a life that calls me to give all that I am in the service of your love for the world. It is a life of joy, but also of sacrifice. It is a glorious life, but also one of suffering. It is a life of peace, but also of struggle. Yes, Lord, it is a life in water and blood, but no longer water and blood that destroy, but water and blood that come from your heart and so bring reconciliation and peace.

I adore you, Jesus, as I look up at you whom they have pierced. Let the blood and water that flow from your heart give me a new heart to live a new life. I know that in this world water and blood will never be separated. There will be peace and anguish, joy and tears, love and agony. They will be there always— together—leading me daily closer to you who give your heart to my heart.

O, Lord Jesus, I thank you. I praise you. I love you. May our hearts be one so that the world may recognize that it is you who sent me, not to condemn, but to offer your heart to all who search for love.

III

"Look, here are my hands . . ."

In the evening of that same day, the first day of the week, the doors were closed in the room where the disciples were, for fear of the Jews. Jesus came and stood among them. He said to them, "Peace be with you," and, after saying this, he showed them his hands and his side. The disciples were filled with joy at seeing the Lord. . . .

Thomas, called the Twin, who was one of the Twelve, was not with them when Jesus came. So the other disciples said to him, "We have seen the Lord," but he answered, "Unless I can see the holes that the nails made in his hands and can put my finger into the holes they made, and unless I can put my hand into his side, I refuse to believe." Eight days later the disciples were in the house again and Thomas was with them. The doors were closed, but Jesus came in and stood among them.

"Peace be with you," he said. Then he spoke to Thomas, "Put your finger here; look, here are my hands. Give me your hand; put it into my side. Do not be unbelieving any more but believe." Thomas replied, "My Lord and my God!" Jesus said to him:

"You believe because you can see me. Blessed are those who have not seen and yet believe."

—John 20:19–20, 24–29

Dear Lord Jesus,

You, eternal Word of the Father, God from God, Light from Light, one in being with the Father, you showed me your divine love by taking on human flesh, living our human life and dying a human death—a death on a cross. But your love is stronger than death. Your divine love breaks through the prison of death and destruction and becomes manifest again in your risen body. O Lord, who will ever be able to understand the heart in which your divine love became flesh! Again I look at you. You rose from the dead, and now you appear to me. You say to me, "Peace be with you," and you show me your wounded hands and your wounded side. Yes, the wounds of your cross are visible on your risen body. I look up at you and know that the marks of your totally self-giving love have found forever a place in the glorified body with which you are ascending to your Father and mine.

Now I see that all those whom you hold in your heart—suffering men and women from every age and from every place on this earth—are lifted up with you, not only on your cross, but also in your resurrection and thus are given here and now a place in your kingdom where you live with the Father and the Holy Spirit for ages unending. Now I see that, even though we are still struggling in this world, we are already one with you as you intercede for us with your Father. Where your heart is, there we are, children of your heavenly Father. In your heart we are forever hidden and present to God. Your heart is our permanent home, our resting place, our refuge and our hope.

Lord Jesus, as I look at the wound in the side of your glorified body and try to enter into the mystery of your resurrection, I am painfully aware of the timidity, the fear and the doubt that fill my own heart. Even though everything is accomplished in you, even though you carry all of humanity within your heart, even though you love me without limit and keep me safe in that love, I live as though there were something important to be found outside of you. I know where my home is. I know where I can safely dwell. I know where I can listen to the voice of love. But still I am restless, searching for what only you can give.

Jesus, look at me in my struggle and show me your compassion. You cry out, "Let anyone who is thirsty come to me! Let anyone who believes in me come and drink!" But I hesitate and feel pulled in so many directions.

Often I act as though you are not visible enough, not audible enough, not tangible enough. The world around me is so easy to see, to hear and to touch, and, before I fully realize it, I am already seeing, hearing and touching with much greed and lust—always asking for more and never fully satisfied. And, as I run away from you, pulled by the colors, sounds and substance of my surroundings, I accuse you for not being concrete enough, and I say what your own disciple Thomas said, "Unless I can put my hands in his side, I refuse to believe."

O, dear Jesus, why can't I simply trust you and the many ways in which you have already shown me your love? Who had the privilege of knowing about you from the moment he could know? I did! Who had parents, friends and teachers radiating your affection and care? I did! Who had so many opportunities to know you better and love you more? I did! And still I remain sulky and unconvinced, saying, "Unless I can put my hands in his side, I refuse to believe."

You are so patient, Lord. You are not angry or resentful. You stand there, take my hand and say, "Put your hand into my side. Do not be unbelieving any more, but believe." Over and over again you take my hand and put it into your wounded side. For a long time I felt jealous of your disciples who saw your pierced side when you appeared to them, and of Thomas who was allowed to touch your wounds. Often I thought, "How much easier would it have been to believe in you and give myself to you without reservation if I could just have been there with them!" But even as I think this way, I know already that I am fooling myself and looking for an excuse to keep my distance from you.

O dear Jesus, your broken heart is so visible and so touchable if I but take the risk of trusting you completely. You are so close to me if I am but willing to open the eyes you have given me. You say to me, "What you have done to the least of mine, you have done to me." The hungry, the thirsty, the naked, the prisoners, the refugees, the lonely, the anguished, the dying, they are all around me and show me your broken heart. I see you every time I walk down the streets, every time I watch television or listen to the radio, every time I open a newspaper, every time I pay attention to a woman, a man or a child who comes to me. I see you every time I let my eyes see the pain of all those with whom I live day after day. You are so close, closer than I ever knew before I looked at your pierced side. You are in my house, on my street, in my town, in my country. You are where I walk and where I sit, where I sleep and where I eat, where I work and where I play. You are never far from me.

O Lord Jesus, this is not a sentimental thought. Oh no, it is a very tangible reality. You who drew all people to yourself as you were lifted up in your pain and in your glory, you stay with us as the wounded and risen Lord. Whenever I touch your broken heart, I touch the hearts of your broken people, and whenever I touch the hearts of your broken people, I touch your heart. Your broken heart and the broken heart of the world are one.

O Lord, it is true. I know it. Every time I overcame the fear of my own wounds and the wounds of those around me and dared to touch them gently, joy and peace came to me in ways I never dreamed of. Sometimes it was just sitting in silence and letting my loneliness be; sometimes it was just listening to a stranger who revealed his anguish to me; sometimes it was waiting with a lonely woman until death set her free; sometimes it was looking in silence at a Rembrandt painting with a friend; sometimes it was crying many tears while holding on to someone who was not afraid of me. O Lord, so often did I wander away to safe places—high, powerful, prestigious and quite visible. But often I felt a strange isolation there as though people around me had become puppets and you a distant stranger. But every time I chose again to turn back to your heart, my own heart started to burn, and an undefinable peace came to me, a peace emerging from the wounds I touched.

Lord Jesus, you always call me closer to your wounded heart. There you want me to know true joy and true peace. Gradually I realize that in your heart, seeing and not seeing, hearing and not hearing, touching and not touching are not contradictions. To Thomas who heard your voice, saw your wounds and touched your pierced side, you said, "You believe because you can see me. Blessed are those who have not seen and yet believe." There, O dear Lord, is the mystery of your love. I have not seen you and yet I truly see you every time I look at the broken bodies of my fellow human beings. I have not heard you, and yet I truly hear you every time I hear the cries uttered by men, women and children in pain. I have not touched you, and yet I truly touch you every time I touch all those who come to me in their loneliness. In the midst of all the human brokenness and human pain, I see, hear and touch the heart of humanity, your humanity, the humanity of all the people embraced by your love.

Thank you, Jesus, for your heart. Thank you for showing me your heart. Thank you for letting me see while not seeing, hear while not hearing, touch while not touching. Thank you for letting me believe more every day, hope more every day and love more every day.

My heart is little, fearful and very timid. It will always be so. But you say, "Come to my heart. My heart is gentle and humble and very broken like yours. Do not be afraid. Come and let your heart find rest in mine and trust that all will be well." I want to come, Jesus, and be with you. Here I am, Lord, take my heart and let it become a heart filled with your love.

Epilogue

On March 28, 1988, the same day I went to the Trappists, Madame Pauline Vanier celebrated her ninetieth birthday with the l'Arche community in Trosly. Two years ago, when I stayed in her house, she often said to me, "What is so hard for me is never to be able again to go to my beloved Canada and visit my children and friends there." At that time, her health was fragile, and, indeed, it seemed that it would be too strenuous for her to make such a journey.

But she soon grew stronger, and, in the fall of 1986, she was able to make a visit to Montreal and spend a couple of days with her Trappist son, Benedict, in his monastery at Oka. When she returned to France, she thought that this had been her last trip to Canada. But it was not. On April 12, two weeks after her birthday celebration, she flew from Paris to Toronto and stayed for five days at Dayspring, a house of prayer at the Daybreak community, which had recently been opened to offer members of l'Arche in North America a place to deepen their spiritual life.

As I wrote my prayers to the heart of Jesus, I suddenly realized that these prayers could be my birthday gift for Mammie. So my secretary, Connie Ellis, typed them, put them together as a small book and placed them on the table of her Dayspring room along with some flowers and a welcome letter.

I wrote her how grateful I was that she had come to Dayspring and expressed my deep regret that I could not be there myself. About the prayers, I said somewhat apologetically, "I wrote these prayers to the heart of Jesus from my heart, encouraged by your constant reminders. They are simple prayers. I didn't feel that I could write a book about the heart of Jesus before knowing how my own heart would speak. I hope that you will accept these prayers as a sign of my love for Jesus and of my deep gratitude to you who led me closer to his heart."

When I called her by phone, she thanked me for the prayers and said, "You know, my eyes are so bad that I cannot read them, but I hope someone will speak them for me on a tape so I can listen to them." I said, "Maybe I can put them on tape for you, but I really wish that someone would simply read them to you."

A few days later, Sue Mosteller, who for fourteen years has helped to give shape to the Daybreak community and who now is the director of Dayspring, read the first prayer to Mammie. Shortly after that, she called me and said, "Henri, this is it! Don't polish it up. It comes from your heart, and it is all about the heart of Jesus. I am moved, thank you, thank you."

As I listened to her trembling voice, the same tremble that I heard when she first asked me to write, a feeling of deep gratitude rushed through me. Something had happened that I had never expected to happen. Something in me, something in her, and something between us: something new that came from the heart of Jesus, something deeply healing. We had very few words to say to each other on the phone. We both knew that God's heart is so infinitely greater than our own and that silence is often better than words.

Sue read all three prayers to her. Shortly after that, Mammie left Dayspring to visit her Trappist son and be with some friends in Montreal. Then she returned to France, to her house in Trosly.

As I think about that house and picture her room in my mind, I see there the icon of John leaning against the breast of Jesus, and I know that both Mammie and I now look at it with new eyes.

I hope and pray that all who will pray these prayers with us will also experience the healing and renewing love that flows from the heart of Jesus.

Henri J.M. Nouwen is one of the most popular spiritual writers of our time. He wrote more than forty books, among them best-selling *With Open Hands* and *Out of Solitude*. He taught at Yale University, Harvard University, and the University of Notre Dame. From 1986 until his death in 1996, he taught and ministered to physically and mentally challenged men and women as a member of the L'Arche Daybreak community in Toronto, Canada. Learn more about Nouwen's life and works at www.henrinouwen.org.

More from Henri J.M. Nouwen

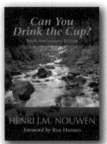

Can You Drink the Cup?
Foreword by Ron Hansen
Henri J.M. Nouwen reflects upon the metaphor of the cup, using the images of holding, lifting, and drinking to articulate the basics of the spiritual life.

ISBN: 1-59471-099-6 / 128 pages / $10.95
Ave Maria Press

With Open Hands
Foreword by Sue Monk Kidd
Henri J.M. Nouwen's first book on prayer. For over thirty years *With Open Hands* has gently encouraged readers to an open, trusting stance toward God and offered insight to the components of prayer: silence, acceptance, hope, compassion, and prophetic criticism. Half a million copies in print in seven languages!

ISBN: 1-59471-064-3 / 128 pages / $9.95
Ave Maria Press

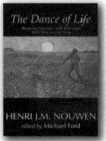

The Dance of Life
Weaving Sorrows and Blessings into One Joyful Step
Edited by Michael Andrew Ford
Spiritual refreshment and guidance through the darkness, loneliness, and turmoil of life's challenges.

ISBN: 1-59471-087-2 / 224 pages / $12.95
Ave Maria Press

Out of Solitude
Three Meditations on the Christian Life
Foreword by Thomas Moore
Invites us to reflect on the tension between our desire for solitude and the demands of contemporary life.

ISBN: 0-87793-495-9 / 64 pages, with photos / $7.95
Ave Maria Press

Available from your bookstore or from
ave maria press / Notre Dame, IN 46556
www.avemariapress.com / Ph: 800-282-1865
A Ministry of the Indiana Province of Holy Cross

Keycode: FØAØ1Ø7ØØØØ